*We hope this book has been informative and helpful on your journey to understanding and celebrating older adults. Thank you for your interest and support!*

*Title: Politics and Governance-The Anatomy of Political Power in the Capitals*

*Subtitle: The Political History of Each Capital*

Series: Cosmopolitan Chronicles: Tales of the World's Great Cities

By Kelli Tempest

*"The world is a book, and those who do not travel read only one page."*
Saint Augustine

*"A city is not gauged by its length and width, but by the broadness of its vision and the height of its dreams."*
Herb Caen

*"The purpose of life is to live it, to taste experience to the utmost, to reach out eagerly and without fear for newer and richer experience."*
Eleanor Roosevelt

*"The only way to do great work is to love what you do."*
Steve Jobs

*"Travel makes one modest. You see what a tiny place you occupy in the world."*
Gustave Flaubert

*"Cities were always like people, showing their varying personalities to the traveler. Depending on the city and on the traveler, there might begin a mutual love, or dislike, friendship, or enmity."*
Roman Payne

*"The best way to predict the future is to create it."*
Abraham Lincoln

*"The world is a beautiful book, but of little use to him who cannot read it."*
Carlo Goldon

*"In every walk with nature, one receives far more than he seeks."*
John Muir

# Table of Contents

# Introduction
## Understanding the role of politics and governance in shaping cities

Cities are complex organisms, shaped by numerous forces such as geography, culture, economics, and politics. However, politics and governance are arguably the most significant forces that shape cities, as they determine how resources are allocated, how decisions are made, and how power is exercised.

Politics refers to the process by which individuals and groups compete for power and influence, while governance refers to the systems and structures through which decisions are made and implemented. Together, politics and governance form the foundation of how cities are run and how they develop over time.

Understanding the role of politics and governance in shaping cities is essential for several reasons. First, it provides insights into how and why cities are developed in particular ways, which can help policymakers and urban planners make informed decisions about future development.

Second, it highlights the importance of civic engagement and participation in politics and governance. When citizens understand how politics and governance work, they are better equipped to engage with the system and advocate for their interests.

Third, it sheds light on the challenges and opportunities that arise when politics and governance intersect with other forces such as culture, economics, and geography. For example, political decisions about infrastructure investment may impact economic growth and social equity in a particular neighborhood or region.

In this book, we will explore the intricate relationship between politics, governance, and the development of capital cities around the world. Through our investigation of different political systems, governance structures, historical events, political players, political economies, and public policies, we aim to provide readers with a deeper understanding of the role that politics and governance play in shaping cities.

We hope that this book will serve as a valuable resource for policymakers, urban planners, scholars, and anyone interested in understanding the dynamics of politics and governance in capital cities. By studying the intricate relationship between politics, governance, and cities, we can develop a more nuanced understanding of how cities are developed, and how they can be improved for the benefit of all citizens.

# The significance of studying politics and governance in capital cities

Capital cities are often the political and administrative centers of their respective countries. They are where important decisions are made, policies are formulated, and resources are allocated. As such, studying the politics and governance of capital cities is essential for understanding how a country is run and how decisions are made that impact its citizens.

In this section, we will explore the significance of studying politics and governance in capital cities. We will highlight the key reasons why it is important to understand how politics and governance work in these cities and what implications this has for policymakers, urban planners, and citizens.

1. Understanding National and Global Politics

Capital cities are often the epicenter of national politics. They are where major decisions are made regarding national policies, legislation, and governance structures. By studying the politics and governance of capital cities, we can gain a deeper understanding of the national political landscape and how it impacts citizens across the country.

Furthermore, capital cities are often centers of global politics as well. They are where important international institutions such as the United Nations, World Bank, and International Monetary Fund are headquartered. By understanding the politics and governance of capital cities, we can gain insights into how global politics and international relations impact our daily lives.

2. Assessing the Effectiveness of Government

Studying the politics and governance of capital cities is essential for assessing the effectiveness of government. By examining how policies are formulated, decisions are made, and resources are allocated, we can evaluate the quality of governance in a particular city or country.

Furthermore, by comparing different capital cities, we can identify best practices and areas for improvement. This can inform policymaking and lead to more effective and efficient governance.

3. Promoting Civic Engagement

Studying the politics and governance of capital cities can also promote civic engagement. When citizens understand how politics and governance work, they are better equipped to engage with the system and advocate for their interests.

Moreover, by examining the role of civil society in governance, we can identify opportunities for citizen engagement and participation. This can lead to a more inclusive and democratic political system.

4. Understanding the Intersection of Politics, Governance, and Urban Development

Finally, studying the politics and governance of capital cities is essential for understanding the intersection of politics, governance, and urban development. By examining how political decisions impact urban development, we can identify opportunities for sustainable and equitable development.

Moreover, by exploring the challenges and opportunities that arise when politics and governance intersect with other forces such as culture, economics, and geography, we can develop a more nuanced understanding of how cities are developed and how they can be improved for the benefit of all citizens.

In conclusion, studying the politics and governance of capital cities is essential for understanding how countries are run and how decisions are made that impact citizens. By examining different political systems, governance structures, historical events, political players, political economies, and public policies, we can develop a more nuanced understanding of the role that politics and governance play in shaping cities. This knowledge can inform policymaking, promote civic engagement, and lead to more effective and equitable urban development.

This book is an exploration of the political and governance systems that shape the world's capital cities. It is designed to provide readers with a comprehensive understanding of the complex and interconnected processes that govern urban life.

In the following pages, we will delve into the different forms of government, the administrative and bureaucratic structures, the historical events and milestones, the political players and ideologies, the relationship between politics and the economy, and the major policy areas that impact each capital city. Through this exploration, we aim to provide readers with a holistic understanding of the anatomy of political power in the capitals.

Chapter 1: Political Systems In this chapter, we will examine the different forms of government that exist in capital cities, including democracies, monarchies, and dictatorships. We will look at the historical development of political systems in each city, compare political systems across cities, and discuss the challenges and opportunities presented by each political system.

Chapter 2: Governance Structures In this chapter, we will explore the administrative and bureaucratic structures of each capital city. We will identify the key institutions and decision-making bodies, analyze the role of civil society in governance, and examine the issues and challenges in governance structures.

Chapter 3: Political History In this chapter, we will delve into the historical events and milestones that have shaped the political landscape of each city. We will analyze the impact of key political figures on the city's development, compare political histories across cities, and extract lessons learned from historical events.

Chapter 4: Political Players In this chapter, we will investigate the current political leaders in each capital city and their ideologies. We will assess the influence of political parties, the role of interest groups and lobbying, and the impact of public opinion and the media on shaping politics.

Chapter 5: Political Economy In this chapter, we will examine the relationship between politics and the economy in each city. We will analyze the impact of economic policies on the city's development, assess the effects of political corruption on the economy, and compare political economies across cities.

Chapter 6: Public Policy In this chapter, we will identify the major policy areas in each capital city, such as education, health, and social welfare. We will analyze the key policy initiatives and their outcomes, assess the role of the public in policy-making, and discuss the challenges and opportunities in public policy implementation.

Chapter 7: Future of Politics and Governance In this chapter, we will investigate the emerging trends and issues in politics and governance in each city. We will assess possible scenarios and future developments, provide recommendations for improving politics and governance in capital cities, and analyze the implications of future developments for the global political landscape.

Conclusion In this concluding chapter, we will summarize the key themes and findings of the book, reflect on the significance of understanding the role of politics and governance in capital cities, and provide final thoughts on the implications of the book's content for readers.

In summary, this book is a comprehensive and detailed exploration of the complex and interconnected processes that govern urban life. It is intended for readers who seek to gain a deeper understanding of the anatomy of political power in the world's capital cities. Whether you are a student of political science, a practitioner of public policy, or simply an engaged citizen, this book will provide you with a wealth of knowledge and insight into the workings of the global political landscape.

# Chapter 1: Political Systems
## Different forms of government in capital cities

Capital cities are the political centers of nations, where decisions that affect the lives of millions of people are made. The form of government adopted by a country influences how decisions are made and the extent of power exercised by the government. This chapter will explore the different forms of government in capital cities, their historical development, challenges, and opportunities.

Democracy

Democracy is a form of government that emphasizes the rule of the people. In democratic societies, citizens are given the right to elect their leaders and participate in the decision-making process. The power of the government is limited by a constitution, which serves as a guide for government actions. Many capital cities, such as Washington D.C. (USA), London (UK), and Tokyo (Japan), are democracies.

Autocracy

Autocracy is a form of government where power is concentrated in the hands of a single leader or a small group of people. Autocracies are characterized by a lack of political freedom, suppression of opposition, and the concentration of power. Some of the capital cities that are autocracies include

Beijing (China), Moscow (Russia), and Riyadh (Saudi Arabia).

Monarchy

Monarchy is a form of government where the head of state is a monarch, such as a king or a queen. The monarch has significant powers, although this is often limited by a constitution. Capital cities with monarchies include London (UK), Stockholm (Sweden), and Madrid (Spain).

Republic

A republic is a form of government where the head of state is elected by the people or their representatives. In some republics, the head of state has significant powers, while in others, the role is largely ceremonial. Some capital cities that are republics include Paris (France), Rome (Italy), and Seoul (South Korea).

Federal System

A federal system of government is one where power is shared between a central government and regional governments. In a federal system, the regional governments have some degree of autonomy and can make decisions that affect their regions. Some capital cities that operate a federal system include Berlin (Germany), Brasilia (Brazil), and Canberra (Australia).

Conclusion

In conclusion, this chapter has explored the different forms of government in capital cities. While each form of government has its advantages and disadvantages, the most important aspect of any government is its ability to serve its citizens effectively. The next chapter will examine the administrative and bureaucratic structures of capital cities.

# Historical development of political systems in each city

The historical development of political systems in each capital city provides valuable insights into the evolution of the city's governance structures, political culture, and socio-economic development. In this chapter, we will explore the historical context in which each city's political system emerged and evolved, identifying key events and factors that shaped the development of their political systems.

Washington D.C. The political system of Washington D.C. has undergone significant changes over the years. Originally, the city was governed by a federally appointed board of commissioners, but in the early 1970s, the Home Rule Act granted the city limited self-governance. Since then, the city has had an elected mayor and city council, with limited powers to pass local laws and budgets. However, the city's unique status as the capital of the United States means that many important decisions about the city's governance are still made at the federal level.

London London's political system has a long and complex history, dating back to the Roman occupation of Britain. Over the centuries, the city has been governed by a variety of institutions, including the monarchy, the church, and the guilds. In the 19th century, the introduction of representative democracy led to the creation of a city council, and in the 20th century, the Greater London Council was established to oversee the city's affairs. However, the GLC was abolished in the 1980s, and since then, the city has been governed by a complex network of local councils, government agencies, and private sector organizations.

Tokyo Tokyo's political system has been shaped by Japan's unique history and culture. Following Japan's defeat in World War II, the country underwent significant political and social reforms, including the adoption of a new constitution that established a parliamentary system of government. Tokyo, as the capital of Japan, has played a central role in these developments, and today, it is governed by a governor and a metropolitan assembly. However, the city's political system is also influenced by traditional Japanese values, such as consensus-building and deference to authority.

Beijing Beijing's political system is shaped by China's long and complex history, as well as the country's recent economic and political developments. Since the founding of the People's Republic of China in 1949, Beijing has been the political and cultural center of the country, and it has been governed by the Communist Party of China. Today, the city is governed by a mayor and a municipal people's congress, and it is home to many of China's most important political institutions, including the National People's Congress and the State Council.

In conclusion, the historical development of political systems in each capital city is shaped by a complex mix of historical, cultural, and political factors. By understanding the unique context in which each political system emerged, we can gain valuable insights into the challenges and opportunities facing each city today.

### Comparison of political systems across cities

Comparing political systems across different capital cities can provide valuable insights into the strengths and weaknesses of different models of government. In this chapter, we will examine the similarities and differences between political systems in various capital cities, and explore the implications of these differences for governance and public policy.

One of the key factors that distinguishes political systems in different cities is the level of decentralization or centralization of power. Some cities have a highly centralized government, with most decision-making authority vested in a single leader or group of leaders, while others have more decentralized systems, with power distributed among multiple levels of government and a range of elected officials and appointed bureaucrats.

Another important factor is the level of participation and representation afforded to citizens. Some political systems prioritize the participation of citizens in decision-making, while others are more hierarchical and top-down in their approach. Some cities have systems that are characterized by high levels of transparency and accountability, while others are more opaque and prone to corruption.

A third factor that influences political systems is the historical context in which they developed. For example, some political systems have evolved gradually over time, while others have been imposed by external powers or have undergone radical transformations as a result of social or political upheaval.

To illustrate these differences and similarities, we will compare the political systems of several capital cities, including Washington D.C., London, Beijing, Brasilia, and New Delhi. We will examine the historical development of each city's political system, the key institutions and decision-making bodies, and the challenges and opportunities associated with each system.

For example, in Washington D.C., the political system is characterized by a high degree of decentralization, with power distributed among multiple levels of government and a range of elected officials and appointed bureaucrats. In contrast, Beijing has a highly centralized system, with most decision-making authority vested in a single leader, the General Secretary of the Communist Party of China. London has a mixed system, with a relatively decentralized government at the local level, but a highly centralized system at the national level.

By comparing these different political systems, we can gain a deeper understanding of the factors that shape governance in capital cities, and the ways in which different models of government can impact public policy outcomes. This chapter sets the stage for the rest of the book, by providing a framework for understanding the similarities and differences between political systems in different capital cities, and the implications of these differences for governance and public policy.

# Challenges and opportunities of each political system

Political systems can present a wide range of challenges and opportunities for the cities they govern. In this chapter, we will explore some of the key challenges and opportunities associated with different political systems in capital cities.

1. Challenges of Political Systems

1.1. Democratic Political Systems Democratic political systems are characterized by the principle of popular sovereignty, which means that power rests with the people. While this can provide citizens with greater freedom and representation, it can also pose several challenges. For instance, democratic political systems can be slow to make decisions, as they require consensus-building and can be vulnerable to gridlock. Additionally, there is always a risk of corruption and abuse of power, as politicians may be swayed by special interests or other factors.

1.2. Authoritarian Political Systems Authoritarian political systems, in contrast, are characterized by a strong central government with limited citizen participation in decision-making. While this can provide for faster and more efficient decision-making, it can also pose several challenges. For instance, authoritarian political systems can be prone to corruption and abuses of power, as there is less transparency and accountability. Additionally, citizens may have limited freedoms and opportunities for political expression.

1.3. Federal Political Systems Federal political systems are characterized by a division of power between a central government and regional governments. While this can provide for greater regional representation and decision-making, it can also pose challenges. For instance, there may be disagreements between different levels of government, leading to inefficiencies and delays. Additionally, there may be challenges in coordinating policy across different regions.

2. Opportunities of Political Systems

2.1. Democratic Political Systems Democratic political systems provide opportunities for citizen engagement and representation. In these systems, citizens have greater freedom of speech, assembly, and association, which can facilitate greater participation in decision-making. Additionally, democratic political systems can foster innovation and creativity, as individuals are encouraged to express their ideas and pursue their interests.

2.2. Authoritarian Political Systems Authoritarian political systems provide opportunities for strong and decisive leadership. In these systems, decisions can be made quickly and efficiently, without the need for consensus-building or debate. This can allow for greater stability and predictability in government decision-making. Additionally, authoritarian political systems can facilitate rapid economic growth, as leaders can make decisions that prioritize economic development over other concerns.

2.3. Federal Political Systems Federal political systems provide opportunities for greater regional representation and decision-making. In these systems, regional governments can tailor policies to the specific needs and priorities of their regions, while the central government can provide coordination and support. Additionally, federal political systems can facilitate cooperation and collaboration between different regions, leading to greater economic development and innovation.

In conclusion, each political system presents its own unique challenges and opportunities. By understanding these factors, we can gain a deeper understanding of the ways in which political systems shape the development and governance of capital cities.

## Chapter 2: Governance Structures
### The administrative and bureaucratic structures of each capital city

The administrative and bureaucratic structures of each capital city play a critical role in shaping its political landscape. In this chapter, we will explore the various administrative and bureaucratic structures that exist in different capital cities and their impact on governance.

Administrative structures vary greatly from city to city, depending on the form of government in place. In some cities, the administrative structure is highly centralized, with power concentrated in the hands of a few key decision-makers. In other cities, power is more widely distributed, with different branches of government playing distinct roles.

In many capital cities, the administrative structure is heavily influenced by historical factors. For example, in London, the administrative structure has evolved over centuries, with different institutions and governing bodies emerging at different points in time. Similarly, in Washington D.C., the administrative structure is heavily influenced by the United States' federal system, with power divided between the federal government and the District of Columbia.

One important aspect of administrative structures in capital cities is the role of civil servants. Civil servants play a critical role in implementing government policies and programs, and their actions can have a significant impact on the city's governance. In some cities, civil servants are highly professionalized and independent, with strict rules governing their conduct. In other cities, civil servants may be subject to political pressure or corruption, leading to inefficiencies or abuses of power.

Bureaucratic structures in capital cities are similarly diverse. In some cities, bureaucratic structures are highly hierarchical, with clear lines of authority and strict rules governing decision-making. In other cities, bureaucratic structures may be more fluid, with decision-making processes evolving over time in response to changing circumstances.

Another important aspect of bureaucratic structures is the role of institutions and decision-making bodies. In some cities, these bodies may be highly centralized, with power concentrated in a few key institutions. In other cities, decision-making power may be more widely distributed, with different institutions playing distinct roles.

In examining the administrative and bureaucratic structures of different capital cities, it is important to consider the challenges and opportunities that these structures present. For example, highly centralized administrative structures may be more efficient in certain contexts, but may also be more prone to abuse of power. Similarly, highly professionalized civil services may be more effective in implementing government policies, but may also be less responsive to changing circumstances.

Overall, understanding the administrative and bureaucratic structures of different capital cities is critical to understanding their political systems and governance structures. In the next chapter, we will examine the key institutions and decision-making bodies that exist in different capital cities, and their role in shaping governance.

### Key institutions and decision-making bodies

Key institutions and decision-making bodies play a crucial role in the governance structures of capital cities. These bodies are responsible for making important decisions that affect the lives of citizens and the direction of the city's development. In this section, we will explore the key institutions and decision-making bodies in different capital cities and how they function.

One of the most important decision-making bodies in many capital cities is the city council or the equivalent governing body. The city council is responsible for creating and enforcing laws, regulations, and policies that govern the city. The council is usually made up of elected officials who represent different parts of the city, and they work together to make decisions that benefit the entire community.

In addition to the city council, there are often other key institutions that are responsible for decision-making in different areas of governance. For example, there may be a separate board or commission responsible for overseeing the city's finances, public utilities, or transportation systems. These bodies are often composed of experts in the relevant fields who are appointed by the city council or other governing bodies.

Another important institution in many capital cities is the mayor's office or the equivalent executive body. The mayor is responsible for overseeing the city's day-to-day operations, implementing policies and initiatives, and representing the city to other levels of government and the public. The mayor is often assisted by a team of advisors and administrative staff who help to manage the various departments and functions of the city.

Aside from the city council and executive bodies, civil society organizations also play an important role in decision-making in many capital cities. These organizations may include advocacy groups, non-governmental organizations, and community-based organizations, among others. They often work to hold government officials accountable, advocate for the needs and interests of marginalized communities, and provide critical services and support to residents.

It is important to note that the administrative and bureaucratic structures of each capital city may vary widely depending on the specific political system in place. For example, in some cities, there may be a strong central government that exerts significant control over local decision-making, while in others, there may be a more decentralized system that gives more power to local communities and neighborhood organizations. The degree of transparency and accountability in decision-making may also vary widely, depending on the level of corruption, political polarization, and civic engagement in each city.

Overall, understanding the key institutions and decision-making bodies in each capital city is crucial for understanding how governance structures function and how decisions are made. By analyzing these structures, we can gain insights into the strengths and weaknesses of different political systems and identify opportunities for reform and improvement.

# The role of civil society in governance

Civil society plays a vital role in the functioning of governance structures in capital cities around the world. Civil society refers to the collection of non-governmental organizations, social movements, and other groups that operate outside of the government and are involved in the public sphere. These organizations can influence and shape governance in various ways. This chapter will discuss the role of civil society in governance and its impact on the political landscape of capital cities.

Firstly, it is important to understand the various forms of civil society that exist in capital cities. These include non-governmental organizations, community-based organizations, labor unions, and other interest groups. These organizations play an important role in representing the interests of citizens and advocating for their rights. They provide a platform for citizens to participate in the political process and hold elected officials accountable.

Civil society also plays a crucial role in monitoring and scrutinizing government policies and actions. Through research, monitoring, and advocacy, civil society organizations can highlight issues and challenge policies that may be detrimental to citizens. They can also provide alternative policy proposals and collaborate with governments to implement policies that are more inclusive and effective.

Another important function of civil society is to provide a voice for marginalized groups and communities. In many capital cities, marginalized groups such as ethnic and religious minorities, women, and the LGBT community face discrimination and exclusion from the political process. Civil society organizations can advocate for the rights of these groups and provide a platform for their voices to be heard.

Furthermore, civil society can act as a check on government power and ensure accountability. By engaging in monitoring and evaluation of government policies and actions, civil society organizations can identify instances of corruption, mismanagement, or abuse of power. They can also hold elected officials accountable by mobilizing public opinion and advocating for reforms.

Despite these positive contributions, civil society faces various challenges and constraints. In many countries, governments may restrict the activities of civil society organizations through laws, regulations, or harassment. Funding for civil society organizations may also be limited, making it difficult for them to carry out their activities effectively. Moreover, civil society organizations may be fragmented or lack coordination, which can limit their impact.

In conclusion, civil society plays a crucial role in governance structures in capital cities around the world. Through advocacy, monitoring, and mobilization, civil society organizations can contribute to more inclusive and effective governance. However, they also face challenges and constraints that can limit their impact. It is therefore essential to create an enabling environment for civil society to operate freely and effectively, and for governments to work collaboratively with civil society to address the challenges facing their societies.

## Issues and challenges in governance structures

While governance structures in capital cities are designed to promote transparency, accountability, and efficiency, they are not immune to issues and challenges that can compromise their effectiveness. In this chapter, we will explore some of the common issues and challenges faced by governance structures in capital cities.

1. Corruption Corruption is one of the major challenges facing governance structures in capital cities. It is the abuse of power for personal gain, and it can occur in different forms, such as embezzlement, bribery, and nepotism. Corruption undermines the rule of law, weakens the trust of citizens in the government, and impedes economic development. Corruption can occur at all levels of government, from low-level bureaucrats to high-level politicians.

2. Political Interference Political interference is another challenge faced by governance structures in capital cities. It occurs when politicians or political parties interfere with the work of government institutions, such as the judiciary, civil service, and regulatory bodies. Political interference can lead to a lack of independence, bias, and inefficiency in the decision-making process, which can

weaken the credibility of government institutions and the trust of citizens in the government.

3. Lack of Transparency Lack of transparency is a major issue in governance structures in capital cities. It occurs when government institutions fail to provide access to information and data related to their operations and decision-making processes. Lack of transparency can lead to a lack of accountability, corruption, and citizen mistrust. It can also limit the effectiveness of civil society and the media in holding the government accountable.

4. Bureaucratic Red Tape Bureaucratic red tape is a common challenge faced by governance structures in capital cities. It refers to the excessive regulations, procedures, and paperwork that can delay or obstruct the decision-making process. Bureaucratic red tape can lead to inefficiency, corruption, and a lack of accountability. It can also discourage investment and hinder economic development.

5. Inadequate Resources Inadequate resources are a significant challenge faced by governance structures in capital cities. It refers to the lack of financial, human, and material resources needed to perform their functions effectively. Inadequate resources can lead to a lack of capacity, corruption, and a lack of accountability. It can also

hinder the implementation of public policies and the provision of public services.

6. Limited Citizen Participation Limited citizen participation is a challenge faced by governance structures in capital cities. It occurs when citizens are not involved in the decision-making process and are not given the opportunity to provide feedback or hold the government accountable. Limited citizen participation can lead to a lack of accountability, corruption, and a lack of trust in the government. It can also limit the effectiveness of public policies and the provision of public services.

Conclusion

In conclusion, governance structures in capital cities face a range of challenges that can compromise their effectiveness in promoting transparency, accountability, and efficiency. These challenges include corruption, political interference, lack of transparency, bureaucratic red tape, inadequate resources, and limited citizen participation. It is essential for governments to address these challenges to promote good governance and ensure that citizens' rights and interests are protected.

# Chapter 3: Political History
## Historical events and milestones that have shaped the political landscape of each city

Each capital city has a unique political history that has shaped its current political landscape. In this chapter, we will examine the historical events and milestones that have influenced the development of each capital's political system.

Washington, D.C.

The political history of Washington, D.C. began with its founding as the capital of the United States in 1790. The city was initially designed by Pierre L'Enfant, a French architect, and planner, to be a symbolic representation of the power and authority of the new nation. The first government buildings were constructed during this period, including the White House and the U.S. Capitol.

During the 19th century, Washington, D.C. continued to develop as a political center, with the growth of the federal government and the expansion of the city's infrastructure. The city's political landscape was shaped by the Civil War, which had a significant impact on the city's economy and population.

The 20th century saw further development of Washington, D.C.'s political institutions, including the establishment of the federal bureaucracy and the growth of political lobbying. The Civil Rights movement of the 1960s also had a significant impact on the city's political landscape, with the passage of laws that increased the political power of African Americans in the city.

London

London has a long and complex political history, dating back to the Roman era. The city became a center of power during the medieval period, with the establishment of the monarchy and the development of the city's financial institutions.

During the 17th century, London became a focal point of political conflict, with the English Civil War and the Glorious Revolution leading to significant changes in the country's political system. The 19th century saw the expansion of the British Empire and the growth of London's economic and political power.

The 20th century saw significant changes in London's political landscape, including the establishment of the Greater London Council in 1965 and the transfer of power from central government to the city's elected officials.

Beijing

The political history of Beijing dates back to ancient times, with the city serving as the capital of various dynasties throughout China's history. The city became the capital of the People's Republic of China in 1949, following the Chinese Civil War.

Under Mao Zedong, Beijing's political landscape was shaped by the Cultural Revolution and the establishment of the Communist Party's centralized system of government. The city's infrastructure was also transformed during this period, with the construction of new buildings and public spaces.

In the 1980s and 1990s, Beijing's political landscape shifted towards a more market-oriented system, with economic reforms and the development of private enterprise. However, political control remained firmly in the hands of the Communist Party, with limited space for political dissent.

Comparative Analysis

By comparing the political histories of Washington, D.C., London, and Beijing, we can see the ways in which each city's political system has been shaped by its unique historical context. Each city has faced different challenges and opportunities, leading to different approaches to governance and political organization.

Lessons Learned

By understanding the historical events and milestones that have shaped the political landscape of each city, we can gain valuable insights into the strengths and weaknesses of different political systems. We can also learn from the successes and failures of past political leaders, and apply these lessons to the challenges facing today's political leaders.

# Key political figures and their impact on the city's development

The history of a city is shaped by the people who lead it, and understanding the impact of key political figures is crucial in understanding the city's development. In this chapter, we will examine the impact of notable political figures on the development of each capital city.

In London, Winston Churchill is perhaps the most famous political figure, serving as the Prime Minister of the United Kingdom twice, during World War II and again in the 1950s. His leadership and inspirational speeches were key in rallying the country during the war, and his impact on British politics continues to be felt today. Another notable figure in London's political history is Margaret Thatcher, who served as Prime Minister in the 1980s. Her policies of privatization and deregulation had a significant impact on the British economy, and her leadership style was known for being strong and divisive.

In Paris, Charles de Gaulle is a towering figure in French political history, serving as both the leader of the French Resistance during World War II and as President of France. He is known for his efforts to modernize France and establish its position as a major world power. Another notable figure in Parisian politics is Jacques Chirac, who served as the Mayor of Paris before becoming President of France. His policies focused on urban renewal and improving the quality of life for Parisians, and he was instrumental in securing the 2024 Summer Olympics for the city.

Washington, D.C. has been shaped by a number of key political figures throughout its history as the capital of the United States. George Washington, the first President of the United States, played a critical role in the establishment of the city and the design of its layout. Abraham Lincoln, who served as President during the Civil War, is perhaps the most famous political figure associated with the city, and his Emancipation Proclamation and Gettysburg Address are both widely regarded as among the most important speeches in American history. More recently, Barack Obama, the first African American President of the United States, called Washington, D.C. home during his time in office, and his policies and leadership style had a significant impact on the city.

In Moscow, Vladimir Lenin is a towering figure in Russian political history, serving as the leader of the Bolshevik Party and playing a critical role in the Russian Revolution. His policies and ideology, known as Leninism, had a profound impact on the development of the Soviet

Union and the world more broadly. Joseph Stalin, who succeeded Lenin as the leader of the Soviet Union, was also a key figure in Moscow's political history, and his policies of collectivization and industrialization had a significant impact on the country's development.

In Beijing, Mao Zedong is perhaps the most famous political figure, serving as the founding father of the People's Republic of China and its first Chairman. His policies, known as Maoism, focused on socialist and communist ideals, and his leadership had a significant impact on China's political and economic development. Another notable figure in Beijing's political history is Deng Xiaoping, who served as the leader of China in the 1980s and is known for his policies of economic reform and modernization.

In this chapter, we have examined the impact of notable political figures on the development of each capital city. By understanding their leadership styles, policies, and contributions, we gain a deeper appreciation for the historical and political contexts that have shaped each city.

# Comparative analysis of political histories across cities

In this chapter, we will explore the political histories of the capital cities discussed in this book, and analyze them comparatively. Each city has its unique history that has shaped its political landscape, but there are also similarities and patterns that can be observed when looking at them collectively.

To start with, it is important to note that most of the capital cities in the world have experienced periods of colonization and imperialism, which have significantly influenced their political development. For instance, London, Paris, and Madrid were once the centers of vast empires, and their political histories are intertwined with their colonial past. In contrast, Washington D.C., Canberra, and Brasília are all relatively new cities that were established in the modern era, and their political histories are closely linked to their status as capital cities.

When examining the political histories of each city, it is important to consider key political figures who have played a significant role in shaping the city's development. For instance, in London, Winston Churchill is widely regarded as one of the most influential figures in the city's political history. Churchill was the Prime Minister of the United

Kingdom during World War II and played a critical role in the country's victory over Nazi Germany. In Paris, Charles de Gaulle is another important political figure who left a lasting impact on the city. De Gaulle served as the President of France twice, and his policies contributed to the city's development as a cultural and political center.

Similarly, in Washington D.C., the political history of the city is closely linked to the presidency of George Washington, the first President of the United States. Washington played a pivotal role in establishing the city as the capital of the United States and creating its political institutions. In Canberra, the capital of Australia, Sir Robert Menzies is regarded as one of the most important political figures in the city's history. Menzies served as the Prime Minister of Australia for over 18 years and played a key role in the city's development as a political and administrative center.

In contrast, in Brasília, the political history of the city is relatively brief, given that it was established only in 1960. However, it is still possible to identify key political figures who have contributed to the city's development. One of them is Juscelino Kubitschek, the President of Brazil who oversaw the construction of Brasília and played a critical role in its early political and economic development.

Comparing the political histories of these cities, it is clear that they have all experienced significant political upheavals and changes over time. However, there are also common patterns that can be observed. For instance, many of these cities have experienced periods of authoritarian rule, such as London under the Tudors, Paris during the reign of Louis XIV, and Brasília under the military dictatorship that ruled Brazil from 1964 to 1985. Similarly, many of these cities have also experienced periods of democratic reform, such as London during the Glorious Revolution, Paris during the French Revolution, and Brasília after the end of military rule.

In conclusion, by comparing the political histories of the capital cities discussed in this book, we can gain valuable insights into the factors that have shaped their political landscapes. Although each city has a unique history, there are also common patterns and trends that can be observed. Understanding these patterns can help us to better understand the current political situation in each city and anticipate future developments.

# Lessons learned from historical events

Introduction: The study of political history is crucial to understanding the current state of politics in any given city. By examining the events, figures, and policies that have shaped a city's political landscape, we can gain insights into the challenges and opportunities that it faces today. In this chapter, we will explore the political history of each of the five capital cities and draw lessons from their past experiences.

Historical events and their impact: Each of the five capital cities has a unique political history that has shaped its current state. For example, the founding of Washington D.C. as the capital of the United States was a political compromise that reflected the tensions between the Northern and Southern states in the early days of the republic. The city's layout, with its grand avenues and monumental buildings, reflects the ambitions of early American leaders to establish a capital city that would rival those of Europe.

Similarly, London's political history is shaped by its status as a former imperial power. The city has been the center of British politics for centuries, and its political institutions, such as Parliament and the monarchy, have played a central role in shaping the country's political landscape. The city's history is also marked by periods of social and political upheaval, such as the English Civil War and the Industrial Revolution.

In Tokyo, the political history is marked by the country's transition from feudalism to modernity. The city was established as Japan's capital in the late 19th century, as the country underwent a process of rapid modernization and industrialization. The city's political institutions, such as the Imperial Palace and the Diet, reflect Japan's unique political culture and history.

Comparative analysis of political histories: By comparing the political histories of these cities, we can gain insights into the challenges and opportunities that they face today. For example, the legacy of colonialism has had a lasting impact on the political systems of many former colonies, such as Delhi and Nairobi. The challenge for these cities is to balance the need to address historical injustices with the need to create a stable and effective political system.

In contrast, the political history of Washington D.C. is marked by the struggle for democracy and civil rights. The city's African American population has played a central role in this struggle, with figures such as Martin Luther King Jr. and Marion Barry making significant contributions to the city's political history. Today, the city's political landscape reflects the continuing struggle for representation and equality.

Lessons learned: From the political histories of these five capital cities, we can draw a number of lessons that are applicable to cities around the world. One key lesson is the importance of a strong and independent judiciary, which can provide a check on the power of the executive and legislative branches of government. Another lesson is the need for transparency and accountability in government, which can help to prevent corruption and abuse of power.

Conclusion: By studying the political histories of these five capital cities, we can gain a deeper understanding of the challenges and opportunities that cities face in their political development. By drawing on these lessons, we can work towards creating more effective, inclusive, and accountable political systems that can serve the needs of all citizens.

# Chapter 4: Political Players
## Current political leaders in each capital city and their ideologies

In this section, we will examine the current political leaders in each capital city and their ideologies. The leaders of a city play a critical role in shaping its political landscape and driving policy decisions. It is important to understand their beliefs and goals in order to gain insight into the political dynamics of the city.

1. Washington D.C.

The current political leader of Washington D.C. is Mayor Muriel Bowser. She is a member of the Democratic Party and has been in office since 2015. Bowser is known for her progressive policies on affordable housing, education, and public safety. She has been a vocal critic of President Trump and his administration's policies, particularly on immigration and healthcare.

2. London

The current political leader of London is Mayor Sadiq Khan. He is a member of the Labour Party and has been in office since 2016. Khan is known for his progressive policies on affordable housing, environmental issues, and public transportation. He has been a vocal critic of Brexit and has pushed for London to remain an international hub for business and innovation.

3. Beijing

The current political leader of Beijing is Mayor Chen Jining. He is a member of the Communist Party of China and has been in office since 2016. Chen is known for his focus on environmental issues and has implemented policies to reduce pollution in the city. He has also supported initiatives to promote sustainable development and increase the use of renewable energy.

4. Moscow

The current political leader of Moscow is Mayor Sergei Sobyanin. He is a member of the United Russia party and has been in office since 2010. Sobyanin is known for his focus on infrastructure development and urban renewal. He has overseen the construction of new transportation systems and public spaces, and has implemented policies to improve the city's overall livability.

5. Tokyo

The current political leader of Tokyo is Governor Yuriko Koike. She is an independent politician and has been in office since 2016. Koike is known for her progressive policies on gender equality, environmental issues, and disaster preparedness. She has also promoted initiatives to support small businesses and increase tourism in the city.

6. New Delhi

The current political leader of New Delhi is Chief Minister Arvind Kejriwal. He is a member of the Aam Aadmi Party and has been in office since 2015. Kejriwal is known for his focus on improving public services and infrastructure in the city. He has implemented policies to provide free healthcare and education to residents, and has supported initiatives to reduce air pollution in the city.

7. Canberra

The current political leader of Canberra is Chief Minister Andrew Barr. He is a member of the Australian Labor Party and has been in office since 2014. Barr is known for his focus on economic development and job creation in the city. He has supported initiatives to promote renewable energy and reduce greenhouse gas emissions.

8. Paris

The current political leader of Paris is Mayor Anne Hidalgo. She is a member of the Socialist Party and has been in office since 2014. Hidalgo is known for her progressive policies on sustainable urban development, affordable housing, and public transportation. She has also been a vocal advocate for combating climate change and reducing air pollution in the city.

In conclusion, the current political leaders in each capital city have different ideologies and priorities, but they all play a crucial role in shaping the political landscape of their respective cities. Understanding their beliefs and goals is essential to gaining insight into the political dynamics of each city.

### Political parties and their influence

Political parties are an essential aspect of any democracy, and they play a significant role in shaping the political landscape of capital cities. In this chapter, we will explore the various political parties operating in each capital city and their influence on the political system.

In many capital cities, political parties are the primary means through which citizens engage in politics. Political parties organize themselves around shared ideological or policy goals, and they compete against one another for control of the government. The political party that secures a majority in the legislative assembly or parliament forms the government.

Each capital city has its unique set of political parties, with varying levels of influence. For instance, in Washington D.C., the two dominant political parties are the Democratic Party and the Republican Party. In London, the Labour Party and the Conservative Party are the two primary political parties, while in Tokyo, the Liberal Democratic Party (LDP) has been the dominant political force for over 60 years.

Political parties play an essential role in the functioning of a democracy, as they provide a mechanism for citizens to participate in the political process. Political parties articulate citizens' interests and concerns, and they propose policy solutions to address these issues. Political parties also help citizens make informed choices during elections, as they provide information about the candidates' policy positions and track records.

In some cases, political parties can also act as a hindrance to democratic governance. Political parties can become overly partisan and engage in gridlock, which can prevent the government from functioning effectively. Additionally, political parties may be beholden to special interest groups or powerful individuals, which can undermine the democratic process.

It is essential to understand the political parties operating in each capital city and their influence on the political system. The political parties' influence can be seen in the policies enacted by the government, the selection of political leaders, and the overall political climate of the city.

In recent years, many capital cities have seen the rise of populist political parties, which challenge the established political order. These parties often appeal to citizens who feel left behind by globalization and are dissatisfied with the political establishment. Populist political parties have gained significant support in many capital cities, including Rome, Athens, and Budapest.

In conclusion, political parties are a crucial aspect of democratic governance in capital cities. They provide citizens with a mechanism for participating in the political process, and they influence the policies enacted by the government. However, political parties can also become a hindrance to democratic governance if they become overly partisan or beholden to special interests. It is essential to understand the political parties operating in each capital city and their influence on the political system to have a complete picture of the city's political landscape.

## Role of interest groups and lobbying

Interest groups and lobbying are key components of political systems in many capital cities around the world. These groups represent specific interests or industries and work to influence policymakers to support their goals and objectives. They can play a significant role in shaping public policy, often with considerable success.

In this chapter, we will explore the role of interest groups and lobbying in the political systems of each capital city. We will examine the various interest groups that exist, the issues they prioritize, and the strategies they employ to influence policymakers. We will also look at the impact of lobbying on public policy, and the potential conflicts of interest that may arise.

Interest groups can be broadly categorized into two types: economic and non-economic. Economic interest groups represent businesses, industries, and labor unions, while non-economic interest groups represent social, cultural, and environmental concerns. Economic interest groups tend to be more powerful, with greater financial resources and political clout.

In each capital city, there are numerous interest groups representing a range of interests. For example, in Washington D.C., the National Rifle Association represents the interests of gun owners, while the American Civil Liberties Union advocates for civil liberties and human rights. In London, the Confederation of British Industry represents the interests of businesses, while Greenpeace advocates for environmental protection.

Interest groups use a variety of strategies to influence policymakers, including direct lobbying, grassroots mobilization, and media campaigns. Direct lobbying involves meeting with policymakers to discuss issues and propose policy solutions. Grassroots mobilization involves rallying supporters to contact policymakers and express their views on a particular issue. Media campaigns involve generating public support for a particular issue through social media, advertising, and other forms of media.

Lobbying can have a significant impact on public policy. Policymakers rely on interest groups for information and expertise on particular issues, and often look to them for guidance on policy decisions. However, lobbying can also create conflicts of interest and undermine the democratic process. Lobbyists may represent narrow interests at the expense of the broader public interest, and may use their financial resources to gain undue influence over policymakers.

Overall, interest groups and lobbying play a crucial role in the political systems of many capital cities around the world. By understanding their influence and the potential risks and benefits they pose, policymakers can make more informed decisions and ensure that the public interest is being served.

**Public opinion and the media in shaping politics**

The role of the media and public opinion cannot be overstated in the modern political landscape. In capital cities, where the concentration of media outlets is usually the highest, the media can have a significant impact on shaping public opinion and influencing political outcomes. This chapter will explore the ways in which the media and public opinion shape politics in various capital cities, and the role that different media outlets play in shaping the narrative around political events.

Media Landscape in Capital Cities

In most capital cities, the media landscape is highly competitive, with many different media outlets vying for attention and readership. This competition can lead to sensationalism and an overemphasis on political scandals, as media outlets try to outdo each other in terms of attracting readers and viewers. However, it can also lead to a healthy marketplace of ideas, with different perspectives and voices represented in the media.

The media landscape can also be heavily influenced by government policies and regulations. In some countries, governments control a significant portion of the media, either through direct ownership or through regulatory bodies that can limit or control what can be published or broadcast.

In other countries, the media is largely independent, although it may still be subject to certain regulations and laws.

Public Opinion and Political Outcomes

Public opinion can play a significant role in shaping political outcomes, especially in democratic countries where politicians must ultimately answer to the electorate. In capital cities, where political decisions are often made at the national level, public opinion can be even more influential. Politicians must be attuned to the concerns and priorities of their constituents, and must work to ensure that their policies align with public opinion.

However, public opinion can also be fickle and subject to change, especially in an era of social media and rapid news cycles. A politician who is popular one day may find themselves facing a backlash the next, as public opinion shifts in response to new information or events. This can make it challenging for politicians to plan and implement long-term policies that may be unpopular in the short term.

Media and Political Narrative

The media can play a significant role in shaping the political narrative around a particular event or issue. By highlighting certain facts and downplaying others, media outlets can influence public opinion and frame the debate in a particular way. This is particularly true in the age of social media, where stories can quickly go viral and shape public opinion before all the facts are known.

In capital cities, where politics is often a high-stakes game, media outlets can be particularly influential in shaping the narrative. Politicians and political operatives may attempt to manipulate the media in order to present a certain image or message to the public. This can lead to a situation where the media becomes complicit in promoting a particular political agenda, rather than serving as an impartial watchdog.

Conclusion

The media and public opinion are powerful forces in shaping politics, especially in capital cities where the concentration of media outlets is high. While the media can play an important role in promoting transparency and holding politicians accountable, it can also be subject to manipulation and bias. Public opinion, while important in a democratic society, can also be fickle and subject to rapid shifts. Understanding the role of the media and public opinion in shaping politics is essential for anyone interested in studying capital cities and their political systems.

# Chapter 5: Political Economy
## The relationship between politics and the economy in each city

The relationship between politics and the economy in each capital city is a complex and intricate one that can have a significant impact on the development and growth of the city. In this chapter, we will examine the various ways in which politics and the economy are intertwined in each of the capital cities featured in this book.

Tokyo:

Japan's economy is often seen as a model for other countries, and Tokyo is at the center of this economic powerhouse. The Japanese government plays a significant role in shaping the country's economy, with policies and regulations that aim to promote growth and development. In particular, the Japanese government has a strong focus on innovation and technology, with policies aimed at supporting research and development in various industries. Additionally, Tokyo is home to some of the world's largest financial institutions, including the Tokyo Stock Exchange and the Bank of Japan.

London:

As one of the world's leading financial centers, London's economy is heavily influenced by the financial industry. The British government plays a significant role in regulating this industry, with policies aimed at maintaining the city's status as a global financial hub. The government also plays a role in promoting other industries, such as technology and tourism. In recent years, London has been affected by Brexit, with uncertainty surrounding the country's future relationship with the EU having an impact on the city's economy.

Washington D.C.:

As the capital city of the world's largest economy, Washington D.C.'s economy is heavily influenced by the policies of the federal government. The U.S. government plays a significant role in shaping the country's economy through various policies and regulations, including tax policies, trade policies, and monetary policy. Additionally, Washington D.C. is home to numerous international organizations, such as the World Bank and the International Monetary Fund, which can have a significant impact on the global economy.

Beijing:

China's economy has undergone significant changes in recent years, with the government playing a major role in shaping the country's economic development. The Chinese government has implemented various policies aimed at promoting economic growth, such as investment in infrastructure and technology. Beijing is home to many of the country's leading companies and research institutions, with a focus on industries such as technology, finance, and manufacturing.

Comparative Analysis:

While each of the four capital cities featured in this chapter has a unique relationship between politics and the economy, there are also some commonalities across them. In each city, the government plays a significant role in shaping economic policy and promoting growth and development. Additionally, all four cities are home to significant financial and technological institutions, which have a significant impact on the global economy.

Challenges and Opportunities:

While the relationship between politics and the economy can be a source of strength and stability, it can also present challenges and opportunities. In each of the capital cities featured in this chapter, there are ongoing debates about the appropriate role of government in the economy, as well as concerns about issues such as income inequality and economic instability. At the same time, there are also opportunities for growth and development in emerging industries, such as technology and renewable energy.

Conclusion:

In conclusion, the relationship between politics and the economy in each capital city featured in this chapter is complex and multifaceted. While the government plays a significant role in shaping economic policy and promoting growth and development, there are also ongoing debates and concerns about the appropriate role of government in the economy. By understanding these relationships and the challenges and opportunities they present, we can gain a better understanding of the economic and political landscape of each of these cities.

# Economic policies and their impact on the city's development

In this chapter, we will examine the economic policies and their impact on the development of each capital city. Economic policies are an important aspect of a country's political system, and they play a crucial role in shaping the economic landscape of a city.

First, we will provide an overview of the economic policies in each capital city. This will include an analysis of the government's role in the economy, such as the degree of intervention in the market, the taxation system, and the regulatory framework. We will also look at the country's trade policies, including tariffs, import and export restrictions, and international trade agreements.

Next, we will examine the impact of these policies on the city's development. We will analyze the economic growth rates, levels of income inequality, and access to basic services like healthcare and education. We will also look at the performance of key economic sectors, such as manufacturing, services, and agriculture, and how they have been affected by government policies.

We will then compare the economic policies of the different cities, highlighting their strengths and weaknesses. We will analyze how each city has approached economic development, the degree of success achieved, and what lessons can be learned from their experiences.

Additionally, we will look at the challenges faced by each city in implementing effective economic policies. These challenges can include corruption, political instability, lack of resources, and a poorly educated workforce. We will also examine the impact of external factors, such as global economic trends and natural disasters, on the economic development of the cities.

Finally, we will discuss the future prospects of each city's economy, and how government policies can be adjusted to ensure sustainable growth and development. This will include an analysis of potential economic opportunities, such as new industries or emerging markets, and how the government can promote innovation and entrepreneurship. We will also examine potential challenges to economic growth, such as climate change and global economic uncertainty, and how governments can prepare for these challenges.

Overall, this chapter will provide a comprehensive analysis of the economic policies and their impact on the development of each capital city, as well as the challenges and opportunities for future economic growth.

## Political corruption and its effects on the economy

Political corruption is a major issue that can have devastating effects on a country's economy. When government officials or politicians abuse their power for personal gain, it can lead to a wide range of economic problems, including reduced foreign investment, increased costs for businesses, and diminished public trust in the government.

In this chapter, we will explore the topic of political corruption and its effects on the economy in the context of the five capital cities.

Definition of Political Corruption Political corruption is defined as the use of power by government officials or politicians for illegitimate private gain. This can take many forms, including bribery, embezzlement, nepotism, cronyism, and patronage.

Effects of Political Corruption on the Economy The effects of political corruption on the economy can be devastating. Here are some examples:

1. Reduced Foreign Investment Foreign investors are often reluctant to invest in countries where political corruption is prevalent. They fear that their investments will not be safe, and that government officials will demand bribes or kickbacks in exchange for contracts or permits. This can

lead to reduced foreign investment and slowed economic growth.

2. Increased Costs for Businesses Businesses that operate in countries with high levels of political corruption often face higher costs. This is because they may have to pay bribes to government officials to obtain licenses, permits, or contracts. These extra costs can make it difficult for businesses to compete, and can reduce their profits.

3. Diminished Public Trust in the Government When citizens perceive that their government officials are corrupt, they may lose faith in the government and become less likely to pay taxes or follow regulations. This can lead to reduced revenue for the government and a weakened economy.

Examples of Political Corruption in Capital Cities Here are some examples of political corruption in each of the five capital cities:

1. Washington D.C. Washington D.C. has a history of political corruption, dating back to the days of Tammany Hall. In recent years, there have been several high-profile cases of corruption, including the conviction of former mayor Marion Barry for drug possession and the indictment of former congressman Jesse Jackson Jr. for misusing campaign funds.

2. London London has also experienced political corruption. In 2012, former London mayor Ken Livingstone was accused of accepting bribes from a property developer in exchange for favorable treatment. More recently, there have been allegations of corruption in the London Metropolitan Police, including claims that officers accepted bribes from journalists.

3. Beijing China has a reputation for high levels of political corruption, and Beijing is no exception. In recent years, there have been several high-profile cases of corruption, including the conviction of former Communist Party leader Bo Xilai for corruption and the investigation of former security chief Zhou Yongkang.

4. Brasilia Brazil has a long history of political corruption, and Brasilia is no exception. In recent years, there have been several high-profile cases of corruption, including the impeachment of former president Dilma Rousseff and the conviction of former president Luiz Inacio Lula da Silva for corruption.

5. Canberra Australia is generally considered to have low levels of political corruption, but there have still been some notable cases in Canberra. In 2015, former speaker of the House of Representatives Bronwyn Bishop resigned after

it was revealed that she had claimed taxpayer-funded expenses for a helicopter ride to a party fundraiser.

Conclusion Political corruption is a serious problem that can have devastating effects on the economy. It reduces foreign investment, increases costs for businesses, and diminishes public trust in the government. By understanding the effects of political corruption, we can work to prevent it and build stronger, more stable economies.

# Comparative analysis of political economies across cities

In this section, we will compare the political economies of the five capital cities discussed in this book, focusing on their similarities and differences in terms of economic policies, industries, and trade.

Economic policies

Each of the five capital cities has a unique set of economic policies that reflect their political systems, governance structures, and historical context. However, there are some commonalities in their approach to economic development. For example, all five cities prioritize attracting foreign investment, promoting entrepreneurship and innovation, and investing in education and infrastructure.

In terms of specific economic policies, there are notable differences among the five cities. For example, City A has a strong focus on free trade and open markets, with few barriers to foreign investment and trade. This has led to the development of a thriving export-oriented manufacturing industry, as well as a booming financial sector. City B, on the other hand, has a more interventionist approach to economic development, with a focus on developing domestic industries and protecting local businesses. This has led to the growth of a diverse range of industries, including high-tech manufacturing, creative industries, and tourism.

City C has a mixed economy, with a balance between state-owned enterprises and private businesses. The government has invested heavily in infrastructure and education, and has also implemented policies to promote domestic consumption and reduce income inequality. City D has a market-oriented economy, with a focus on developing a competitive business environment and attracting foreign investment. The government has implemented policies to promote innovation and entrepreneurship, and has also invested in infrastructure and education.

Finally, City E has a socialist-oriented economy, with a strong emphasis on state-owned enterprises and central planning. The government controls many key industries, such as energy and telecommunications, and has implemented policies to promote social welfare and reduce income inequality.

Industries

The industries that dominate each city's economy reflect their unique economic policies and comparative advantages. City A is known for its manufacturing industry, particularly in electronics and textiles. The city is home to several large multinational corporations, and its export-oriented manufacturing sector accounts for a significant portion of its GDP.

City B has a diverse range of industries, including high-tech manufacturing, creative industries, and tourism. The city is home to several well-known tech companies, as well as a thriving film and television industry. Its natural beauty and cultural attractions also make it a popular destination for tourists.

City C's economy is dominated by state-owned enterprises in key industries such as energy, transportation, and telecommunications. The city also has a significant manufacturing industry, particularly in heavy machinery and equipment.

City D has a rapidly growing technology sector, with several high-profile startups and established tech companies. The city is also home to a thriving financial industry, with a large number of banks and investment firms.

City E's economy is dominated by state-owned enterprises, particularly in energy, transportation, and telecommunications. The government also places a strong emphasis on agriculture, and the city is known for its production of rice and other crops.

Trade

The five capital cities have varying degrees of openness to international trade. City A is the most open, with a strong focus on free trade and few barriers to foreign investment and trade. The city is a major exporter of manufactured goods, particularly electronics and textiles.

City B has a more protectionist approach to trade, with a focus on developing domestic industries and protecting local businesses. The city has implemented policies to promote import substitution and reduce dependence on foreign goods.

City C has a mixed approach to trade, with a balance between state-owned enterprises and private businesses. The city has implemented policies to promote both import and export, and has also invested in developing infrastructure to facilitate trade.

City D is highly dependent on international trade, particularly in technology and financial services. The city has implemented policies to promote exports and attract foreign investment, and has developed a highly skilled workforce to meet the demands of these industries. The city's economic policies have focused on creating a favorable business environment, with low taxes and regulations, and a strong emphasis on innovation and entrepreneurship. City D has also invested heavily in infrastructure, such as airports,

ports, and high-speed railways, to facilitate international trade and commerce. As a result, the city has experienced rapid economic growth and has become a global center for technology and finance.

In contrast, City E has a highly regulated economy with significant government control and ownership of key industries, such as energy and telecommunications. The city's economic policies prioritize social welfare and equity, with high taxes and a robust welfare system. While this approach has led to a more equal distribution of wealth, it has also resulted in slower economic growth and lower levels of foreign investment. City E's infrastructure is also less developed than City D, with fewer international airports and seaports, and limited investment in high-speed railways.

Comparing the economic policies and structures of City D and City E highlights the different approaches that cities can take to promote economic growth and development. While City D's emphasis on creating a favorable business environment has led to rapid economic growth and global competitiveness, City E's focus on social welfare has resulted in a more equal distribution of wealth but lower levels of foreign investment and slower economic growth. These examples demonstrate that there are trade-offs between economic growth and social welfare, and cities must carefully consider their economic policies to balance these competing priorities.

## Chapter 6: Public Policy
### Major policy areas in each capital city, such as education, health, and social welfare

Public policies are a vital aspect of any government's functioning, as they reflect its priorities and values. In this chapter, we will examine the major policy areas in each of the capital cities, namely, education, health, and social welfare.

Education is an essential aspect of any society's development, and each capital city has implemented policies to improve the quality and accessibility of education. City A, for example, has made significant strides in providing universal access to education and investing in educational infrastructure. The city has also implemented policies to address inequality in education, such as increasing funding for schools in disadvantaged areas and providing financial assistance to low-income families.

City B has focused on improving the quality of education, particularly in STEM fields, to meet the demands of the city's rapidly growing technology sector. The city has implemented policies to encourage innovation in education, such as establishing public-private partnerships to fund research and development in educational technology.

In City C, education policies have focused on promoting diversity and inclusivity in schools. The city has implemented programs to address discrimination in education and ensure that all students have access to high-quality education, regardless of their background.

Health is another critical policy area, and each capital city has implemented policies to promote public health and provide healthcare services to its citizens. City A, for example, has implemented policies to address the issue of healthcare inequality, such as increasing funding for public hospitals and providing financial assistance to low-income families.

City B has focused on promoting preventive healthcare and healthy lifestyles. The city has implemented policies to encourage physical activity and healthy eating, such as establishing community gardens and public parks and providing incentives for companies to offer wellness programs to their employees.

In City C, health policies have focused on addressing the specific health needs of different population groups, such as the elderly and people with disabilities. The city has implemented policies to provide healthcare services tailored to these groups' needs, such as establishing geriatric care centers and providing home healthcare services.

Social welfare is another critical policy area, and each capital city has implemented policies to address social inequality and provide assistance to vulnerable populations. City A has implemented policies to address poverty and unemployment, such as providing financial assistance to low-income families and offering job training programs.

City B has focused on promoting social mobility and upward mobility. The city has implemented policies to provide access to education and job opportunities, such as establishing scholarship programs for low-income students and partnering with companies to offer job training and employment opportunities to underprivileged groups.

In City C, social welfare policies have focused on addressing social isolation and loneliness, particularly among the elderly. The city has implemented policies to provide social support and opportunities for social engagement, such as establishing community centers and organizing social events for the elderly.

Overall, each capital city has its unique set of policy priorities, reflecting its values and priorities. Despite the differences in policy areas and approaches, each city shares a common goal of improving the lives of its citizens and promoting social, economic, and political development.

### Key policy initiatives and their outcomes

Public policy initiatives are a critical aspect of governance in any city, with the primary aim of improving the quality of life of citizens. In this section, we will discuss some of the key policy initiatives implemented in each of the capital cities and their outcomes.

In City A, the government has focused on improving the quality of education by investing in infrastructure, teacher training, and curriculum development. The city has seen a significant improvement in the quality of education, with a higher number of students graduating from high school and enrolling in college. In addition, the government has implemented policies to support small and medium-sized enterprises (SMEs), including tax breaks and easier access to financing. These policies have led to an increase in entrepreneurship and the creation of new jobs.

City B has focused on improving healthcare services, particularly for the elderly and vulnerable populations. The city has implemented policies to expand healthcare coverage, improve hospital facilities, and enhance healthcare infrastructure. These initiatives have led to improved health outcomes, including a decrease in infant mortality rates and an increase in life expectancy. The city has also implemented policies to promote renewable energy and reduce greenhouse gas emissions, resulting in a decrease in the city's carbon footprint.

In City C, the government has implemented policies to address income inequality and poverty. These policies include social welfare programs, such as cash transfer programs, and the provision of basic services such as healthcare and education to underserved communities. These initiatives have led to a reduction in poverty rates and an improvement in the overall well-being of citizens. Additionally, the city has implemented policies to support sustainable tourism, leading to an increase in the number of tourists visiting the city and an increase in revenue.

City D has implemented policies to promote innovation and entrepreneurship, particularly in the technology and financial sectors. The city has established incubators and accelerators to support startups, and it has implemented policies to attract foreign investment. These policies have led to a thriving startup ecosystem, with several successful technology companies emerging from the city. Additionally, the city has implemented policies to improve public transportation, resulting in a decrease in traffic congestion and a more efficient transportation system.

Overall, these policy initiatives demonstrate the commitment of each city's government to improving the quality of life of its citizens. While the specific policies and their outcomes vary across cities, they all reflect the priorities and values of each city's government and its citizens.

## The role of the public in policy-making

The role of the public in policy-making is a crucial aspect of democracy and good governance. It ensures that policies are responsive to the needs and interests of the people and that the decision-making process is transparent and accountable.

There are different ways in which the public can be involved in policy-making, such as through public consultations, town hall meetings, online platforms, and citizen assemblies. These mechanisms provide opportunities for citizens to express their views and opinions, ask questions, and provide feedback on policy proposals.

One example of public involvement in policy-making is the participatory budgeting process. This is a democratic process in which community members directly decide how to allocate part of a public budget. Participatory budgeting typically involves several stages, including idea collection, proposal development, project selection, and implementation.

Another way in which the public can be involved in policy-making is through civil society organizations. These organizations play an important role in advocating for policy changes, promoting public awareness and engagement, and holding governments accountable. Civil society organizations can also provide expertise and resources to support policy development and implementation.

The role of the media is also crucial in engaging the public in policy-making. The media can provide a platform for public discussion and debate on policy issues, disseminate information about policy proposals, and hold governments accountable for their policies and actions.

However, there are also challenges and limitations to public involvement in policy-making. For example, the public may lack the necessary information and resources to participate effectively in policy discussions, and some groups may be excluded from the process. In addition, policy-making processes may be complex and time-consuming, making it difficult for citizens to stay engaged.

Furthermore, there may be political and institutional barriers to public involvement in policy-making, such as resistance from policymakers, lack of funding and resources for public consultations, and limited capacity of civil society organizations.

To address these challenges, it is important to promote transparency, accessibility, and inclusiveness in policy-making processes. This can be done by providing clear and accessible information about policy proposals, engaging a diverse range of stakeholders, and creating opportunities for meaningful participation.

In conclusion, the role of the public in policy-making is a critical aspect of democratic governance. It is important to ensure that policies are responsive to the needs and interests of the people and that the decision-making process is transparent and accountable. While there are challenges and limitations to public involvement in policy-making, there are also opportunities to promote greater participation and engagement, and to strengthen democratic governance at the local, national, and global levels.

# Challenges and opportunities in public policy implementation

Public policy implementation is a complex process that involves multiple actors, institutions, and factors that can hinder or facilitate the achievement of policy goals. In this section, we will discuss the challenges and opportunities in public policy implementation in each capital city.

One of the main challenges in public policy implementation is the lack of political will and commitment to the policy goals. In some cases, political leaders may prioritize short-term political gains over long-term policy outcomes, which can undermine the effectiveness of the policy. In addition, competing interests and conflicting values among different stakeholders can make it difficult to reach consensus on policy implementation.

Another challenge is the capacity and resources of the government to implement policies effectively. Limited financial and human resources can constrain the implementation of policies, particularly in areas such as health, education, and social welfare. In some cases, bureaucratic inefficiencies and corruption can also hinder the implementation of policies.

Furthermore, the effectiveness of public policy implementation can also be influenced by external factors such as globalization, technological change, and demographic shifts. For example, rapid technological change can make it difficult for governments to keep up with the latest developments and adapt policies accordingly.

Despite these challenges, there are also opportunities to improve public policy implementation in each capital city. One key opportunity is the use of technology and innovation to enhance the efficiency and effectiveness of policy implementation. For example, digital platforms and data analytics can help governments to collect, analyze, and disseminate information about policy outcomes, as well as engage with citizens and stakeholders in the policy-making process.

Another opportunity is the collaboration and partnerships between different actors and stakeholders in the implementation of policies. Engaging with civil society organizations, the private sector, and other stakeholders can provide valuable insights and resources to improve policy implementation, as well as increase public accountability and transparency.

Finally, the adoption of evidence-based policy-making can also enhance the effectiveness of policy implementation. By using rigorous research and data analysis, governments can identify the most effective policy interventions and allocate resources more efficiently.

In conclusion, public policy implementation is a complex and challenging process that requires political commitment, adequate resources, and effective governance structures. While there are many challenges in implementing policies, there are also opportunities to enhance the effectiveness of policy implementation through the use of technology, collaboration, and evidence-based policy-making.

# Chapter 7: Future of Politics and Governance Emerging trends and issues in politics and governance in each city

As the world rapidly changes, cities face new challenges and opportunities in politics and governance. In this chapter, we will examine the emerging trends and issues in politics and governance in each of the four capital cities.

City A: Inclusive Governance

City A has been making strides in promoting inclusivity in its governance structures. With a growing immigrant population, the city has recognized the importance of diversity in decision-making and has implemented policies to ensure that all voices are heard. One of the city's recent initiatives is the establishment of a community advisory board, which brings together representatives from different ethnic and cultural groups to provide input on city policies. The city has also been investing in language services and cultural competency training for its public servants to better serve its diverse population. However, challenges remain in ensuring that all communities have equal access to resources and opportunities.

City B: Technological Advancements

City B has been at the forefront of technological advancements in governance. The city has implemented smart city initiatives, such as the use of data analytics to improve traffic management and the development of mobile apps to enhance citizen engagement. The city has also been investing in artificial intelligence to improve public service delivery and decision-making. However, as the city continues to embrace technology, there are concerns about data privacy and security, as well as the potential for technological advancements to exacerbate existing inequalities.

City C: Climate Change and Sustainability

City C has been taking proactive steps towards addressing climate change and promoting sustainability. The city has implemented policies to reduce carbon emissions, such as promoting the use of electric vehicles and investing in renewable energy sources. The city has also been working towards building more sustainable infrastructure and encouraging sustainable living practices among its citizens. However, the city faces challenges in balancing economic growth with environmental concerns and ensuring that its sustainability initiatives are equitable and benefit all members of the community.

City D: Regional Cooperation

City D has recognized the importance of regional cooperation in addressing common challenges and promoting shared goals. The city has been working closely with neighboring cities and jurisdictions on issues such as transportation, trade, and security. The city has also been involved in regional initiatives to promote economic growth and cultural exchange. However, challenges remain in ensuring that regional cooperation is effective and inclusive, particularly given the diverse political and cultural contexts of the different jurisdictions.

Conclusion

In conclusion, the four capital cities each face unique challenges and opportunities in politics and governance. City A is focused on promoting inclusive governance, City B is embracing technological advancements, City C is addressing climate change and sustainability, and City D is prioritizing regional cooperation. By examining the emerging trends and issues in each city, we can gain insight into the future of politics and governance and the potential for innovative solutions to address complex problems.

## Possible scenarios and future developments

As the world continues to evolve, the future of politics and governance in each capital city is subject to change. Here are some possible scenarios and future developments:

1. Increased use of technology: In the future, technology will play an even more significant role in politics and governance. Governments may use artificial intelligence and big data to analyze and make decisions on policy issues, and citizens may use technology to engage with their elected officials.

2. Greater focus on sustainability: Environmental sustainability is becoming an increasingly pressing issue globally, and it is likely that governments in each capital city will place greater emphasis on sustainability in their policies and decision-making.

3. Changing demographics: The demographics of each capital city are changing, with many becoming more diverse. This will likely result in shifts in political power and changes in policy priorities to reflect the needs of a more diverse population.

4. Increasing globalization: The world is becoming more interconnected, and this will likely impact the politics and governance of each capital city. Governments may need to navigate complex international relationships and trade

agreements, and citizens may demand more global cooperation on issues such as climate change and economic development.

5. Shifts in power dynamics: As countries and regions become more economically and politically powerful, there may be shifts in the balance of power between cities and regions within each country. This could result in changes to the way policies are made and implemented at the national level.

6. Increasing public participation: There is a growing demand for greater public participation in politics and governance. In the future, governments may need to find ways to incorporate citizen input into decision-making processes and be more transparent in their actions.

7. Greater focus on social issues: Social issues such as income inequality, access to healthcare, and affordable housing are likely to remain important policy priorities in the future. Governments in each capital city may need to develop innovative solutions to address these issues and ensure social equity.

8. Changes in political ideologies: Political ideologies are subject to change over time, and the future of politics and governance may be shaped by new and evolving ideologies. For example, the rise of populist movements in some

countries may result in a shift towards more nationalist policies.

In conclusion, the future of politics and governance in each capital city is subject to change as the world continues to evolve. While there are many possible scenarios and future developments, it is clear that technology, sustainability, changing demographics, globalization, shifts in power dynamics, public participation, social issues, and political ideologies are likely to play a significant role in shaping the future of politics and governance in each city. It will be up to the governments, citizens, and other stakeholders in each capital city to navigate these changes and ensure that they are able to meet the needs and expectations of their constituents in the years to come.

# Recommendations for improving politics and governance in capital cities

As we have explored the political and governance landscapes of capital cities, we have identified several areas for improvement. In this section, we will provide some recommendations for policymakers, leaders, and citizens to enhance the effectiveness, accountability, and inclusivity of politics and governance.

1. Strengthening democratic institutions

To ensure the long-term stability and prosperity of capital cities, it is essential to strengthen democratic institutions. This can be achieved by promoting transparency, accountability, and citizen participation in decision-making processes. Some of the specific recommendations include:

- Enforcing stricter campaign finance laws to reduce the influence of money in politics

- Improving the access to information laws to ensure citizens have access to government documents and data

- Providing more opportunities for citizen participation in the policy-making process, such as through town hall meetings, public consultations, and citizen assemblies

- Enhancing the capacity and independence of oversight institutions, such as the judiciary, auditor general, and ombudsman, to ensure checks and balances on the executive branch

- Developing and implementing codes of conduct for elected officials and civil servants to promote ethical behavior and prevent corruption

2. Investing in education and human capital

A well-educated and skilled population is a critical asset for the development and prosperity of capital cities. Investing in education and human capital can help reduce inequality, promote social mobility, and increase economic competitiveness. Some of the specific recommendations include:

- Increasing funding for education, particularly for disadvantaged communities, and expanding access to high-quality education and training opportunities

- Promoting lifelong learning and continuous skill development, particularly in emerging sectors such as technology and green industries

- Encouraging the development of vocational and technical education programs that provide practical skills and certification to meet the needs of the labor market

- Addressing the gender gap in education and promoting gender equality in all areas of society

3. Addressing urban challenges

Capital cities often face significant urban challenges such as congestion, pollution, and housing affordability. Addressing these challenges requires comprehensive and integrated policy approaches that involve multiple stakeholders. Some of the specific recommendations include:

- Promoting sustainable urban planning that prioritizes public transportation, green spaces, and mixed-use development

- Encouraging the adoption of green technologies and practices, such as renewable energy, energy-efficient buildings, and waste reduction and recycling

- Addressing housing affordability by implementing policies such as inclusionary zoning, rent control, and housing subsidies for low-income families

- Engaging in regional cooperation and coordination to address issues such as transportation, housing, and environmental protection

4. Harnessing technology for good governance

The rapid advancement of technology presents both challenges and opportunities for politics and governance. Capital cities can harness technology to enhance transparency, accountability, and citizen engagement. Some of the specific recommendations include:

- Developing open data platforms that provide access to government information and data in a user-friendly format

- Enhancing digital government services, such as online portals and mobile apps, to improve efficiency and accessibility of government services

- Engaging citizens through social media and other online platforms to encourage feedback, participation, and collaboration in policy-making processes

- Ensuring the privacy and security of personal data and preventing the misuse of technology for political purposes

Conclusion

Politics and governance are essential for the well-being and prosperity of capital cities. By implementing these recommendations, policymakers, leaders, and citizens can work together to enhance the effectiveness, accountability, and inclusivity of politics and governance in their cities. It is important to recognize that there is no one-size-fits-all approach, and each city must develop its own unique strategies based on its context, challenges, and opportunities. However, by sharing best practices, learning from each other's experiences, and collaborating across borders, we can build a better future for all capital cities and their inhabitants.

One key recommendation for improving politics and governance in capital cities is to prioritize transparency and accountability. This can involve measures such as strengthening access to information laws, enhancing public consultation processes, and increasing the use of open data and digital platforms to promote greater citizen engagement and participation in decision-making. Additionally, it is crucial to address political corruption and promote ethical behavior among public officials. This can be achieved through measures such as stricter regulations on campaign finance, strengthening anti-corruption agencies, and enhancing transparency in procurement processes.

Another important recommendation is to invest in education and training for policymakers and civil servants. This can help to build the capacity of government institutions and ensure that they have the knowledge, skills, and tools needed to address complex policy challenges. Furthermore, it is essential to foster a culture of innovation and experimentation in governance, by encouraging the use of evidence-based policy-making, promoting collaboration between different sectors and stakeholders, and supporting the development of new technologies and tools to improve the delivery of public services.

Finally, it is important to recognize the interdependence of politics, governance, and economic development, and to adopt a holistic approach to policy-making that takes into account the social, environmental, and economic dimensions of urban life. This can involve measures such as promoting sustainable and inclusive growth, addressing income inequality and social exclusion, and enhancing the resilience of cities to climate change and other global challenges. By adopting a forward-looking, collaborative, and inclusive approach to politics and governance, capital cities can become thriving, resilient, and equitable places that serve the needs and aspirations of all their citizens.

## Implications of future developments for the global political landscape

The future of politics and governance in capital cities has significant implications for the global political landscape. As these cities are often centers of economic and political power, their governance systems and policies can have a ripple effect that extends far beyond their own borders. In this section, we will explore some of the implications of future developments in capital cities for the global political landscape.

One of the most significant implications is the potential shift in the balance of power. As emerging economies continue to grow and become more politically influential, there may be a shift away from the dominance of traditional Western powers. For example, the rise of China as a global economic and political power could lead to a shift in the global balance of power. This shift could have significant implications for international relations and cooperation, particularly in areas such as trade and security.

Another implication is the potential for new models of governance to emerge. As cities grapple with new challenges and opportunities, they may develop innovative approaches to governance that could be emulated by other cities and even countries. For example, cities may adopt new forms of citizen engagement, such as participatory budgeting, to increase accountability and transparency in decision-making. Additionally, cities may experiment with new forms of digital governance, such as blockchain technology, to enhance security and efficiency.

The future of politics and governance in capital cities also has implications for global trends in policymaking. As cities become more prominent players in global politics, there may be a shift towards more decentralized policymaking. This could involve greater collaboration and coordination between cities on issues such as climate change, economic development, and public health. Additionally, there may be a trend towards more evidence-based policymaking, as cities leverage data and technology to inform policy decisions.

The potential for greater international collaboration and coordination among cities also has implications for the role of nation-states in global politics. As cities become more prominent players, nation-states may need to adapt their approaches to diplomacy and governance to reflect this changing landscape. This could involve greater decentralization of power within nation-states, as cities demand more autonomy and control over their own affairs. Additionally, it may involve a shift towards more multilateral forms of diplomacy, as cities work together to address global challenges.

Finally, the future of politics and governance in capital cities has implications for the broader trajectory of global development. As cities become more prosperous and influential, there may be a greater emphasis on urbanization as a driver of economic growth and development. This could lead to greater investment in urban infrastructure and services, such as transportation, housing, and education. However, it could also lead to greater inequalities between urban and rural areas, as cities concentrate wealth and resources.

In conclusion, the future of politics and governance in capital cities has significant implications for the global political landscape. As cities continue to grow and evolve, they will play an increasingly important role in shaping international relations, policymaking, and development. It is therefore crucial that policymakers, leaders, and citizens work together to ensure that these developments are inclusive, sustainable, and beneficial for all.

## Conclusion

## Recap of key themes and findings in the book

The preceding chapters have examined the politics, economy, public policy, and future developments in seven capital cities across the world. This chapter serves as a recap of the key themes and findings in the book, highlighting the similarities and differences in each city's governance and politics.

The first theme is the role of history in shaping the political and economic landscape of each city. The history of a city, including its colonial past, shapes its political and economic institutions, policies, and practices. For example, the legacy of apartheid in Johannesburg continues to influence its social and economic policies, while the authoritarian past of Seoul has led to a strong centralized government.

The second theme is the impact of globalization and regional integration on the political economy of each city. Cities like Singapore and Dubai have leveraged their strategic location and open economies to become hubs for international trade and investment. The political economy of each city is also influenced by its relationship with other cities and regions, as seen in the case of Moscow's dependence on natural resource exports and its ties to other resource-rich cities in the region.

The third theme is the role of political players, including political parties, interest groups, and the media, in shaping politics and policy outcomes. While political parties are important in many cities, interest groups and lobbying play a significant role in shaping policy outcomes in Washington D.C. and Brussels. The media also plays a crucial role in shaping public opinion and influencing policy decisions in cities like London and Tokyo.

The fourth theme is the relationship between politics and the economy, and the impact of economic policies on the development of each city. In many cities, corruption is a significant obstacle to economic development, as seen in the case of Brasilia. However, effective economic policies can promote growth and development, as seen in the case of Seoul's emphasis on innovation and entrepreneurship.

The fifth theme is the importance of public policy in addressing social and economic challenges. Education, healthcare, and social welfare are important policy areas in all cities, and each city has developed its own unique policies and initiatives to address these challenges. However, the role of the public in policy-making varies across cities, with some cities like Berlin having a strong tradition of participatory democracy.

The final theme is the future of politics and governance in each city, and the implications of future developments for the global political landscape. Emerging trends such as the rise of populism and the growth of digital technology will have a significant impact on politics and governance in the future. However, there are also opportunities for innovation and collaboration, as seen in the case of Copenhagen's efforts to become a carbon-neutral city.

In conclusion, this book has explored the politics and governance of seven capital cities across the world, highlighting the similarities and differences in their political and economic institutions, policies, and practices. While there are challenges and obstacles in each city, there are also opportunities for progress and innovation. By learning from each other's experiences and collaborating across borders, we can build more effective, accountable, and inclusive governance systems that promote the well-being and prosperity of all citizens.

## Implications for understanding the role of politics and governance in capital cities

The study of capital cities and their political and governance systems has significant implications for our understanding of how politics operates in modern societies. In this concluding chapter, we recap the key themes and findings of this book and explore their broader implications for the study of politics and governance.

Firstly, this book has demonstrated the importance of understanding the complex relationships between politics, economics, and society in capital cities. Each city has its unique history, culture, and socio-economic conditions, which have shaped its political and governance structures. Therefore, any analysis of these structures must take into account the historical, cultural, and economic context in which they operate.

Secondly, this book has highlighted the critical role that political institutions, such as legislative bodies, bureaucracies, and political parties, play in shaping political outcomes in capital cities. Political institutions can act as a check on executive power, provide opportunities for citizen participation, and facilitate collective decision-making. However, they can also be a source of inefficiency, corruption, and capture by special interests.

Thirdly, this book has shown that political and governance systems in capital cities are constantly evolving in response to changing societal and economic conditions. Therefore, any analysis of these systems must be dynamic and account for the potential for future changes.

Fourthly, this book has emphasized the importance of citizen participation in politics and governance. Citizen participation can increase the accountability of political leaders and institutions, ensure that policies reflect the needs and preferences of citizens, and promote transparency and public trust. However, it is important to recognize that not all citizens have equal access to political participation, and there are significant barriers to entry for certain groups, such as marginalized communities.

Finally, this book has highlighted the importance of global interconnectedness in shaping politics and governance in capital cities. As capital cities become more interconnected through trade, immigration, and other forms of exchange, the policies and governance practices of one city can have significant implications for others.

In conclusion, the study of capital cities and their politics and governance systems has significant implications for our understanding of how politics operates in modern societies. By understanding the complex relationships between politics, economics, and society in these cities, we can develop more effective strategies for addressing political and governance challenges in our own communities.

The significance of this book's content cannot be overstated, as it provides readers with a comprehensive and detailed understanding of the role of politics and governance in capital cities. The book's exploration of the political, economic, and social dynamics of these cities provides readers with valuable insights into how these cities operate and how they are likely to evolve in the future.

One of the most significant contributions of this book is its focus on the interplay between politics and governance. By examining the relationship between these two critical elements, the book offers readers a nuanced understanding of how politics shapes governance and how governance, in turn, influences politics. This understanding is essential for anyone interested in working in or studying the field of politics or public policy.

Another key contribution of this book is its emphasis on the unique characteristics of each capital city. By highlighting the specific political, economic, and social factors that shape each city, the book shows readers the importance of taking a context-specific approach to politics and governance. This insight is particularly relevant for policymakers and practitioners, as it emphasizes the importance of tailoring policies and strategies to the unique needs and challenges of individual cities.

Moreover, the book's exploration of emerging trends and issues in politics and governance is particularly relevant given the ongoing global political and economic changes. By examining the implications of these trends and issues for capital cities, the book provides readers with valuable insights into the challenges and opportunities that lie ahead. This understanding is essential for policymakers and practitioners looking to navigate the rapidly changing landscape of global politics and governance.

Overall, the book's significance lies in its ability to provide readers with a comprehensive and nuanced understanding of the role of politics and governance in capital cities. Its exploration of the interplay between politics and governance, the unique characteristics of individual cities, and emerging trends and issues in politics and governance makes it an invaluable resource for anyone interested in understanding the complex dynamics of these cities.

**THE END**

## Key Terms and Definitions

To help you better understand the language and concepts related to aging and older adults, below you will find a list of key terms and their definitions.

1. Politics: The process of making decisions that apply to members of a group. It involves the use of power, influence, and authority to achieve the goals of the group.

2. Governance: The process of managing the affairs of a group or organization. It involves the creation and implementation of policies, rules, and regulations that guide the behavior of members.

3. Capital city: The city that serves as the center of government and administration for a country or state.

4. Public policy: The decisions and actions taken by governments to address public issues and problems.

5. Public administration: The management of public resources and services, including budgeting, planning, and implementation.

6. Political economy: The study of the relationship between politics and the economy, including the distribution of resources, wealth, and power.

7. Democracy: A political system in which power is held by the people, either directly or through elected representatives.

8. Authoritarianism: A political system in which power is held by a single individual or group, without the consent of the governed.

9. Globalization: The process of increasing interconnectedness and interdependence among countries and regions of the world, including economic, political, and cultural integration.

10. Civil society: The space for collective action and voluntary associations outside of the state and the market.

11. Accountability: The obligation of those in power to provide information, justification, and justification for their actions and decisions.

12. Transparency: The quality of being open, honest, and accessible in the actions and decisions of those in power.

13. Inclusivity: The practice of ensuring that all members of a group are represented and have a voice in decision-making processes.

14. Corruption: The abuse of power for personal gain, often involving the exchange of bribes or kickbacks.

15. Public opinion: The attitudes, beliefs, and values held by members of the public on various issues and topics.

16. Media: The channels of communication used to transmit information and news, including print, television, radio, and the internet.

17. Economic development: The process of improving the standard of living and well-being of individuals and communities through economic growth and expansion.

18. Social welfare: The provision of assistance and support to individuals and communities in need, including healthcare, education, housing, and income support.

19. Education: The process of acquiring knowledge and skills through teaching, training, and research.

20. Health: The state of physical, mental, and social well-being, including access to medical care and services.

Introduction:

- Rosenau, J. N., & Czempiel, E. O. (Eds.). (1992). Governance without government: Order and change in world politics. Cambridge University Press.

Chapter 1: Political Systems

- Dahl, R. A. (1971). Polyarchy: Participation and opposition. Yale University Press.

- Diamond, L. (1992). Economic development and democracy reconsidered. American Behavioral Scientist, 35(4), 450-499.

- Huntington, S. P. (1991). The third wave: Democratization in the late twentieth century. University of Oklahoma Press.

Chapter 2: Governance Structures

- Rhodes, R. A. W. (1997). Understanding governance: Policy networks, governance, reflexivity and accountability. Open University Press.

- Rosenau, J. N. (1992). Governance, order, and change in world politics. In J. N. Rosenau & E. O. Czempiel (Eds.), Governance without government: Order and change in world politics (pp. 1-29). Cambridge University Press.

- Sorens, J. (2013). Good governance and the normative foundations of administrative power. Public Administration Review, 73(4), 625-635.

Chapter 3: Political History

- Anderson, B. (1991). Imagined communities: Reflections on the origin and spread of nationalism. Verso.

- Hobsbawm, E. J. (1990). Nations and nationalism since 1780: Programme, myth, reality. Cambridge University Press.

- Skocpol, T. (1979). States and social revolutions: A comparative analysis of France, Russia, and China. Cambridge University Press.

Chapter 4: Political Players

- Dahl, R. A. (1961). Who governs? Democracy and power in an American city. Yale University Press.

- Evans, P. B. (1995). Embedded autonomy: States and industrial transformation. Princeton University Press.

- Tilly, C. (1975). Reflections on the history of European state-making. In C. Tilly (Ed.), The formation of national states in Western Europe (pp. 3-83). Princeton University Press.

Chapter 5: Political Economy

- Acemoglu, D., & Robinson, J. A. (2012). Why nations fail: The origins of power, prosperity, and poverty. Crown Publishers.

- Berman, S. (2012). The primacy of politics: Social democracy and the making of Europe's twentieth century. Cambridge University Press.

- Stiglitz, J. E. (2002). Globalization and its discontents. WW Norton & Company.

Chapter 6: Public Policy

- Hill, M. (2013). The public policy process. Routledge.

- Howlett, M., & Ramesh, M. (2003). Studying public policy: Policy cycles and policy subsystems. Oxford University Press.

- Majone, G. (1997). From the positive to the regulatory state: Causes and consequences of changes in the mode of governance. Journal of Public Policy, 17(2), 139-167.

Chapter 7: Future of Politics and Governance:

Heywood, A. (2015). Politics. Palgrave Macmillan. (pp. 361-376).

Rhodes, R. A. (2017). Understanding governance: Ten years on. Organization studies, 38(4), 547-574. (pp. 559-567).

Sassen, S. (2018). A savage sorting of winners and losers: Contemporary versions of primitive accumulation. Globalizations, 15(2), 167-180. (pp. 173-177).

Conclusion:

Hirschman, A. O. (1970). Exit, voice, and loyalty: Responses to decline in firms, organizations, and states. Harvard University Press. (pp. 90-104).

Inoguchi, T., & Jain, P. C. (Eds.). (2018). Understanding Asia: Enabling transformation. Springer. (pp. 321-329).

Keohane, R. O., & Nye, J. S. (2011). Power and interdependence revisited. International organization, 65(2), 239-257. (pp. 251-254).